REMARKABLE CANADIANS

Frederick Banting

by Diana Marshall

Published by Weigl Educational Publishers Limited
6325 – 10 Street SE
Calgary, Alberta, Canada
T2H 2Z9

Website: www.weigl.com

Library and Archives Canada Cataloguing in Publication

Marshall, Diana
    Frederick Banting / Diana Marshall.

(Remarkable Canadians)
Includes index.
ISBN 978-1-55388-311-1 (bound)
ISBN 978-1-55388-312-8 (pbk.)

    1. Banting, F. G. (Frederick Grant), Sir, 1891-1941--Juvenile literature.
2. Insulin--History--Juvenile literature. 3. Diabetes--Research--Canada--Juvenile
literature. 4. Physicians--Ontario--Biography--Juvenile literature. I. Title. I. Series.

R464.B3M37 2007   j616.4'62027092   C2006-906253-6

Printed in the United States of America
1 2 3 4 5 6 7 8 9 0 11 10 09 08 07

Editor: Liz Brown
Design: Terry Paulhus

We acknowledge the financial support of the Government of Canada through the Book
Publishing Industry Development Program (BPIDP) for our publishing activities.

Cover: Frederick Banting was the first Canadian to win a Nobel Prize in Medicine.

Photograph Credits:
Cover: The Thomas Fisher Rare Books Library; Lucille Teasdale and Piero Corti
Foundation (Italy): page 13 bottom left; Registered by the Government of Ontario under
the Trade Marks Act: page 7 top left; The Thomas Fisher Rare Book Library, University
of Toronto: pages 1, 5, 6, 8, 10, 14, 15, 16, 17, 18, 19, 20; Victoria University Library
(Toronto), Augusta Stowe-Gullen Collection: page 13 bottom right.

Contents

Who Is Frederick Banting?

Frederick Banting was a doctor and scientist. He was also a war hero and an artist. Frederick is well known for discovering a treatment for **diabetes mellitus**. The treatment was called **insulin**. Before his discovery, people who had diabetes were very ill. Their bodies slowly became sick. With insulin, **diabetics** were able to lead healthier lives. Frederick's discovery was so important that he won the Nobel Prize for Medicine in 1923. In 2004, he was named one of the "Greatest Canadians" by the Canadian Broadcasting Corporation (CBC).

> *"The greatest service in life is that of the medical profession."*

Growing Up

Frederick Grant Banting was born in a farmhouse in Alliston, Ontario, on November 14, 1891. His friends and family called him Fred. There were six children in the Banting family. Fred was the youngest. Fred's brothers were many years older than him. He did not have anyone to play with on the farm. He spent a great deal of time with his pets and the farm animals. He especially liked dogs.

Fred's mother worked in the home. Fred's father was a farmer. He farmed vegetables, fruits, grains, cows, sheep, and pigs. Fred helped his father on the farm. When an animal became ill, Fred and his brothers helped their father **examine** the animal. Fred's interest in research may have begun with these examinations.

❦ Fred and his brothers enjoyed reading and listening to stories each night after supper.

Ontario Tidbits

COAT OF ARMS

BIRD
Common Loon

FLOWER
White Trillium

The Great Lakes are in Ontario.

Niagara Falls is in Ontario. Millions of tourists visit the massive waterfalls each year.

Toronto is the capital city of Ontario. It is the largest city in the country.

Parliament Hill is in Ottawa, Ontario. Ottawa is the capital of Canada.

More than 11 million people live in Ontario.

Think about it!

Fred was born on a farm in Ontario. Research the jobs and chores that people do on farms. How do you think the farm chores that Fred did as a boy influenced his career in medicine?

Practice Makes Perfect

Fred began attending school when he was seven years old. Although he studied a great deal, Fred did not receive good grades. His parents taught him that success was possible with hard work. Even though Fred always tried his best at school, he had to repeat some of his high school exams. In high school, Fred wanted to quit school. However, he did not stop trying. Fred retook the exams and passed them.

When Fred was a teenager, he attended Alliston High School in Alliston.

When Fred finished high school, his parents wanted him to be a **minister**. He wanted to be a doctor. In 1910, Fred began studying religion at Victoria College in Toronto. In 1912, he decided to transfer into the medical school.

In 1915, Fred joined the **Canadian Officers Training Corps**. When he was not studying at school, Fred would march and train for the military.

When Fred turned 21, his father gave him $1,500 as a gift. Fred used this money to help pay for his schooling.

Key Events

In the summer of 1916, Fred finished his medical studies. Canada was fighting in **World War I**, and many soldiers were being injured. The army needed doctors. In 1917, Fred travelled to Europe to help the army. During the war, he was able to practise his skills as a **surgeon**.

Fred returned to Toronto in 1919. He worked at the Hospital for Sick Children. In 1920, Fred moved to London, Ontario, and opened his own **practice**.

To make more money, Fred began teaching at a university. One night, he found it difficult to fall asleep. Fred was thinking about the lesson he was going to teach the next day. The lesson was about diabetes and the **pancreas**. While thinking about the lesson, Fred had an idea about how he could help people with diabetes. This idea would lead him to the discovery of insulin.

🍁 Fred wrote his idea about diabetes in his journal at 2 a.m. on October 31, 1920.

Thoughts from Fred

As a doctor, Fred worked hard to help others. Here are some of the things he said about his life and interests.

Fred's father teaches him to look after the farm animals.

"We always had a share in things...we made or thought we were making our own money and it gave a feeling of independence, responsibility and interest."

Fred wants to begin research on his idea about diabetes.

"I wished to give up practice in London immediately and commence work."

Fred takes up painting as a hobby.

"I knew absolutely nothing about painting and had never seen an artist at work...my happiest hours of this period were thus spent trying to copy pictures...I was very proud of some of them."

Fred talks about his love for hard work.

"I do not know what I would do if I were not busy."

Fred watches a doctor tend to some injured men.

"I watched every movement of those skillful hands as he examined the injured men...From that day it was my greatest ambition to become a doctor."

An idea keeps Fred awake one night. It leads to the discovery of insulin.

"I got up and wrote down the idea and spent most of the night thinking about it."

What Is a Doctor?

Doctors treat sickness and cure diseases. There are many kinds of doctors. Some doctors work with patients to help them heal their bodies. Other doctors help people by learning about the causes of diseases and creating medicines. These doctors are medical scientists.

Frederick Banting worked as a doctor and a medical scientist. Medical scientists ask questions about problems that they see in people's health. Then, they perform experiments. Some experiments take place in a **laboratory**. Medical scientists use what they learn from experiments to create new treatments for illnesses.

🍁 Some doctors become specialists. This means they have special knowledge about one area of medicine.

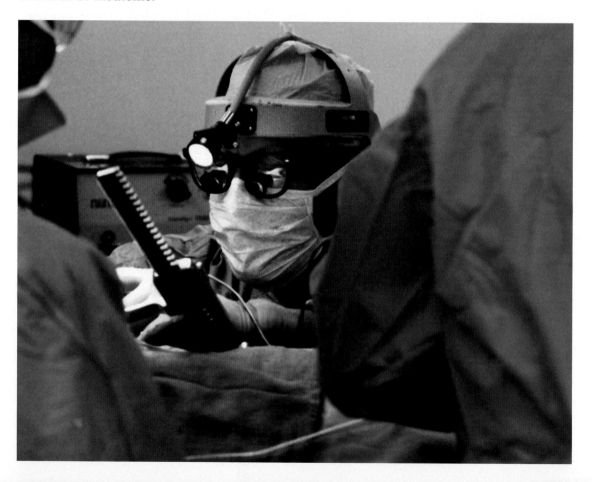

Doctors 101

Henry Norman Bethune (1890–1939)

Field of Study: Surgery, or the treatment of an injury or disease through an operation

Achievements: Bethune invented the movable medical unit. The unit was a portable hospital. This helped him perform surgery on soldiers during battle.

Awards: Accepted into the Canadian Medical Hall of Fame, 1998

Sir William Osler (1849–1919)

Field of Study: Pathology, or the study of diseases and their effects on the body

Achievements: Osler helped open Johns Hopkins Medical School in Baltimore, Maryland. Today, this medical school is one of the best in the world. Osler changed how people learned about medicine. His student doctors trained at hospitals. This gave them experience working with patients.

Awards: Accepted into the Canadian Medical Hall of Fame, 1994

Emily Howard Stowe (1831–1903)

Field of study: Homeopathic medicine, or the treatment of a disease with small amounts of substances, which in large amounts, cause the disease

Achievements: Stowe was the first woman doctor in Canada. She attended medical school in the United States because Canadian medical schools did not accept women in the 1860s.

Awards: Jubilee Medal, 1935; was on a postage stamp, 1981

Lucille Teasdale (1929–1996)

Field of Study: Surgery

Achievements: Teasdale was one of the first female surgeons in Quebec. In 1961, she travelled to Uganda, Africa, to help open a hospital and treat people. This area did not have many doctors. At the hospital, Teasdale helped more than 300 patients each day. Today, the hospital that Teasdale helped open is one of the largest in Uganda.

Awards: Order of Canada, 1991

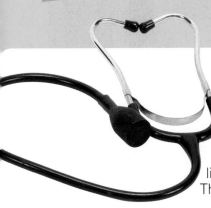

The Stethoscope

Doctors use many tools to discover what is causing sickness or disease in their patients. One of the most important tools for doctors is the stethoscope. The stethoscope was invented by René Laennec in 1816. He was from France. The stethoscope allows doctors to listen to sounds inside the body, such as the heartbeat. This helps doctors **diagnose** illnesses in patients.

Influences

Fred's parents were his strongest influences. Fred's father taught him about responsibility. He taught Fred that hard work leads to success. Fred admired his father, and he loved his mother. He spent a great deal of time with his mother because he was much younger than his brothers.

Fred's parents enjoyed reading books. They taught their children to read so they could learn about the world. Reading and learning were important to Fred. These skills helped him when he studied medicine.

Fred's mother and father were married in 1879.

Living on a farm meant that Fred spent a great deal of time with animals. This taught him to respect and care for animals. When Fred was a doctor, he performed his insulin experiments on dogs. When he was performing experiments, he made the dogs as happy, comfortable, and healthy as he could. He played with them and gave them plenty of care.

Fred's Artistic Influences

Many people in Fred's family were artistic, including Fred. His aunt was a painter. One of Fred's brothers was good at pencil drawings. When Fred was young, he began sketching trees and farm animals. He painted landscapes using oil paints. Painting was Fred's hobby as an adult.

When Fred (right) was an adult, he became friends with the painter, A.Y. Jackson. In 1927, they travelled to the Arctic together to sketch and paint the scenery.

Overcoming Obstacles

When Fred began his medical practice in London, he did not have many patients. Most new doctors begin practising medicine with an experienced doctor who has many patients. Fred did not work with another doctor. He had to find his own patients.

Fred was bored because he had too few patients. He also needed more money. Fred began teaching at the University of Western Ontario. This helped fill his time and gave him more money. While teaching, Fred began thinking about how he could treat diabetes.

After Fred had his idea about diabetes, it took him less than 15 months to discover insulin.

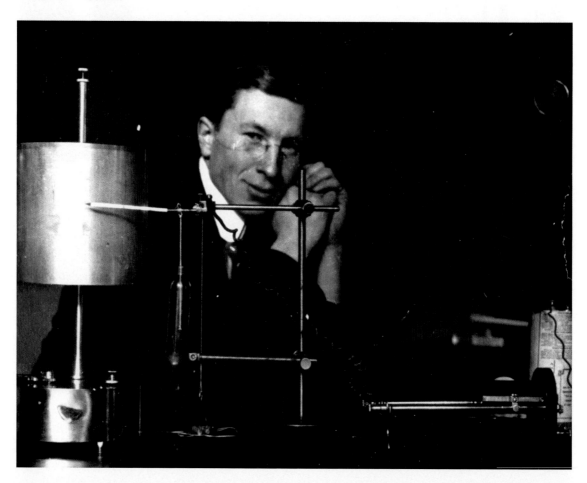

When Fred had his idea, he tried to convince the **chief doctor** at the university to let him conduct experiments. The chief doctor told Fred that the university did not have the proper equipment for his experiments. Fred travelled to the Toronto Medical School at the University of Toronto. At the school, Fred convinced a well-respected doctor that his idea about diabetes was worth researching. The doctor's name was John Macleod. John promised Fred a laboratory, an assistant, and some dogs for his experiments. It was a difficult decision for Fred to leave his practice in London. However, he decided to move to Toronto.

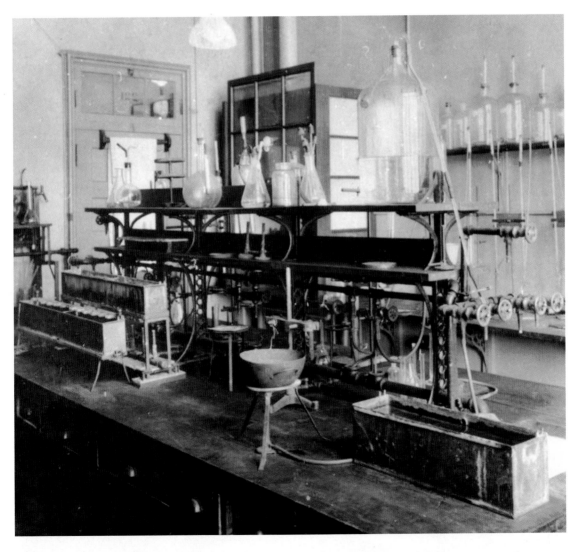

The laboratory where Fred and his assistant, Charles Best, did their research, is nicknamed "the laboratory where insulin was discovered."

Achievements and Successes

Fred achieved much success during his life. He was a talented doctor and a war hero. Fred showed bravery and courage when he saved the lives of injured soldiers in World War I. For his help in World War I, Fred was awarded the Military Cross. This award is given to soldiers who show bravery during battle.

Two years after Fred returned from World War I, he began his diabetes experiments with the help of Charles Best. Fred was a good surgeon, so he performed the operations. In the experiments, Fred and Charles caused dogs to become diabetic. They did this by removing the dogs' pancreas. Then, they tested the dogs' blood for sugar. They tried many different tests. One test was successful. They had given a dog a substance from a **withered** pancreas. This substance was insulin.

Fred's discovery of insulin helped millions of people suffering from diabetes lead healthier lives.

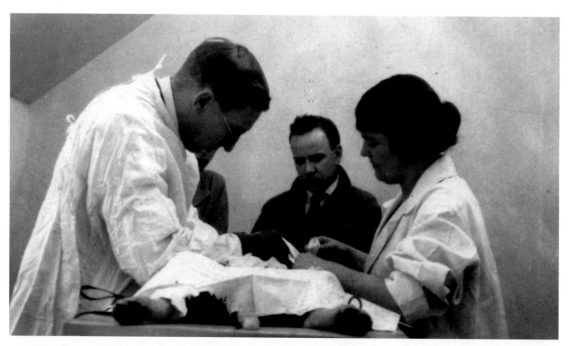

On January 23, 1922, Fred and Charles tested insulin on a human. Fred had found a new way to treat diabetes. In May of the same year, Fred announced that he had made a new discovery. By the end of 1922, diabetics around the world were being treated with insulin. On December 10, 1923, Fred and John won the Nobel Prize in Medicine for his discovery. Fred believed that Charles should have won the award with him, so he gave Charles half of his prize money.

After his discovery, Fred continued to conduct experiments. When **World War II** began in 1939, Fred joined the army again. On February 20, 1941 Fred boarded an airplane. He was travelling to England for the war. Fred did not make it to England. The airplane crashed in Newfoundland. Fred and two other men died in the accident.

The Banting Institute

The University of Toronto named a medical building the Banting Institute to honour Fred. He was given the top floor of the building for his research. Fred's work showed people that research was important for saving lives and improving health. As a result, more people began giving money to support scientists' research.

The Banting Institute opened on September 17, 1930.

Write a Biography

A person's life story can be the subject of a book. This kind of book is called a biography. Biographies describe the lives of remarkable people, such as those who have achieved great success or have done important things to help others. These people may be alive today, or they may have lived many years ago. Reading a biography can help you learn more about a remarkable person.

At school, you might be asked to write a biography. First, decide who you want to write about. You can choose a doctor, such as Frederick Banting, or any other person you find interesting. Then, find out if your library has any books about this person. Learn as much as you can about him or her. Write down the key events in this person's life. What was this person's childhood like? What has he or she accomplished? What are his or her goals? What makes this person special or unusual?

A concept web is a useful research tool. Read the questions in the following concept web. Answer the questions in your notebook. Your answers will help you write your biography.

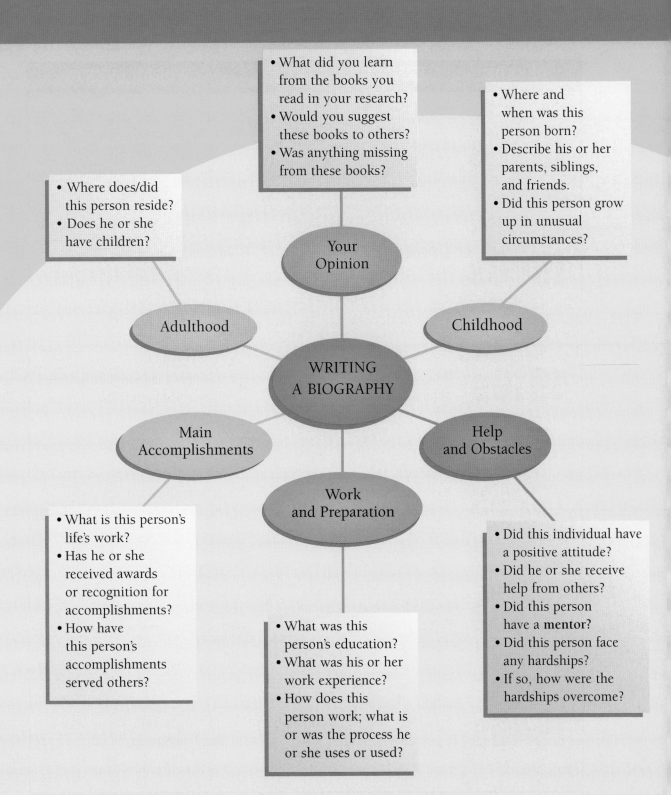

- What did you learn from the books you read in your research?
- Would you suggest these books to others?
- Was anything missing from these books?

- Where and when was this person born?
- Describe his or her parents, siblings, and friends.
- Did this person grow up in unusual circumstances?

- Where does/did this person reside?
- Does he or she have children?

Your Opinion

Adulthood

Childhood

WRITING
A BIOGRAPHY

Main
Accomplishments

Help
and Obstacles

Work
and Preparation

- What is this person's life's work?
- Has he or she received awards or recognition for accomplishments?
- How have this person's accomplishments served others?

- What was this person's education?
- What was his or her work experience?
- How does this person work; what is or was the process he or she uses or used?

- Did this individual have a positive attitude?
- Did he or she receive help from others?
- Did this person have a **mentor**?
- Did this person face any hardships?
- If so, how were the hardships overcome?

Timeline

DECADE	FREDERICK BANTING	WORLD EVENTS
1890s	Fred is born on November 14, 1891, in Alliston, Ontario.	In 1899, Bayer begins selling a pain relief medicine called Aspirin.
1900s	Fred attends Alliston High School.	On December 17, 1903, Orville and Wilbur Wright fly the world's first airplane.
1910s	Fred graduates from medical school on December 9, 1916.	World War I is fought in Europe between 1914 and 1918.
1920s	On May 3, 1922, Fred and his assistant, Charles Best, announce that they have discovered insulin.	Alexander Fleming discovers **penicillin** in 1928.
1930s	Fred is knighted. He becomes Sir Frederick Banting.	Ernst Ruska createst the world's first electron **microscope** in 1931.
1940s	Frederick Banting dies in a plane crash on February 21, 1941.	From 1939 to 1945, World War II is fought in Europe.

Further Research

How can I find out more about Frederick Banting?

Most libraries have computers that connect to a database for researching information. If you input a key word, you will be provided with a list of books in the library that contain information on that topic. Non-fiction books are arranged numerically, using their call number. Fiction books are organized alphabetically by the author's last name.

Websites

To learn more about Sir Frederick Banting, visit www.diabetes.ca/Section_About/bantingIndex.asp

To learn more about Nobel Prize winners, visit http://nobelprize.org

To learn about the other "Greatest Canadians" of the CBC, visit www.cbc.ca/greatest/top_ten

Words to Know

Canadian Officers Training Corps: an organization that trained university students for the military

chief doctor: the doctor in charge of a hospital or univeristy

diabetes mellitus: a serious disease in which a person's body cannot absorb sugar and starch

diabetics: people who have diabetes

diagnose: to identify an illness

examine: look closely to answer questions

insulin: a substance that helps the body break down food

knighted: given a title because of achievement or success

laboratory: a place where scientific work is done

mentor: a wise and trusted teacher

microscope: a tool used by scientists to study very small objects

minister: a leader of a church

pancreas: gland in the body that produces insulin and other substances needed to break down food

Parliament Hill: where the Canadian government makes decisions

penicillin: an antibiotic used to treat many infections

practice: a doctor's business

surgeon: a doctor who treats diseases or injuries by using tools to fix things inside the body

withered: dry and shriveled

World War I: a war fought by many countries between 1914 and 1918

World War II: a war fought between many countries between 1939 and 1945

Index